Big Stuff in the Ocean

Text and photographs by
JOHN
CHRISTOPHER FINE

fulcrum kids

Text and photographs copyright © 1998 John Christopher Fine

Front cover images of dolphin, octopus, and barracuda
copyright © 1998 John Christopher Fine
Back cover images of sea turtle, lobster, and ray
copyright © 1998 John Christopher Fine

Book design by Alyssa Pumphrey

Library of Congress Cataloging-in-Publication Data
Fine, John Christopher.
    Big stuff in the ocean / John Christopher Fine.
        p.   cm.
    Summary: Text and photographs present the habits and behavior of barracudas, dolphins, sea turtles, and other large sea creatures.
    ISBN 1-55591-357-1 (hc.)
    1. Marine animals—Juvenile literature. [1. Marine animals.]
    I. Title.
QL122.2.F55   1998
591.77—dc21   98-18618
                                                CIP
                                                 AC

Printed and Bound in Hong Kong

0 9 8 7 6 5 4 3 2 1
Fulcrum Publishing
350 Indiana Street, Suite 350
Golden, Colorado 80401-5093
(800) 992-2908 • (303) 277-1623
website: www.fulcrum-resources.com
e-mail: fulcrum@fulcrum-resources.com

Contents

Introduction

The more we learn about the big animals that inhabit the deep and often unexplored worlds in the oceans, the more we realize how well adapted and intelligent they are.

What's smart and what's not is a human way of putting things into neat categories. Intelligence for a wild animal has a different meaning than when the term is applied to a human being. A dolphin, after all, does not sit down at a desk and take a math quiz. Dolphins, however, navigate in their own social groups and use echolocation (reflected sound waves) to hunt for food and survive in the wild. Animals must adapt their behaviors to the environment as the acuteness of their senses of sound, smell, and sight often mean the difference between life and death.

We'll take a look at some of the big stuff in the oceans, seas, and coastal areas of the world, and with the help of science and research, we'll learn why some of these animals behave the way they do. With our short exploration into the world's oceans, perhaps we will better understand and appreciate the important role these intelligent ocean dwellers play in our human lives and in the vast life cycle on Earth—a place scientists have come to call Planet Ocean.

The BARRACUDA

Don't wear anything shiny if you are going to dive near barracudas. They have keen eyesight and are attracted to anything that reflects sunlight. They also have large pointed teeth for grasping prey.

Barracudas are long sleek fish that live in tropical seas and oceans. Some species migrate during spawning, which generally occurs from April to September. They glide through the water with just a stroke of their powerful tails. There are about twenty species of barracuda. Some reach 8 feet or more in length, while young barracudas range from about 1 to 3 feet in length.

Barracudas sometimes travel in schools, looking like a solid moving wall to divers. Some lead solitary lives, hunting for their food alone. Anglers cast lines with large hooks near shipwrecks or reefs to hopefully catch a barracuda close to its home, but the lines are frequently broken because of the fish's strength. Divers then find barracudas trailing long stainless-steel leaders with hooks still in their mouths.

While barracudas are predatory fish, hunting their food with powerful jaws and sharp teeth, there are very few attacks on humans reported. Attacks usually occur when a person spears one but only wounds it. Some barracudas have been tamed to take food out of a diver's mouth underwater. No matter how used to divers these fish become, barracudas are still wild animals, and a careless diver can get a nasty bite.

The DOLPHIN

Did you know that all dolphins have teeth? In fact, they belong to a family of marine mammals known as toothed whales. Dolphins range in size from 3 feet long to the 20-foot-long orca or killer whale, the largest member of the dolphin family. However, a dolphin is not a fish. It is an air-breathing mammal that feeds its young with milk, the same way humans do.

Some people call dolphins, porpoises. Translated from Latin, porpoise means "pig fish." In olden days when sailors heard dolphins breathing at the water's surface, they thought the sounds of air going in and out of the dolphins' blowholes were like the noises pigs make.

One of the most popular dolphins is the bottlenose dolphin. Marine aquariums use the bottlenose dolphin in shows, not because they are more intelligent than other dolphins, but because they are known for their winning "smiles"; their natural jawlines turn up in a way that make them seem to always have a happy expression on their faces. Adult bottlenose dolphins can weigh from about 350 to 750 pounds and are very powerful animals.

In the wild dolphins may swim as much as 35 miles a day. They use their tails to move them forward and their flippers to steer and balance them. Their flippers have a five-toed limb-bone structure, just like our own human hands.

Dolphins can dive very deep, even to depths of 1,000 feet and more. When diving, the dolphin's heartbeat slows, oxygen is absorbed more quickly into its muscles, and its lungs are collapsed by the

pressure of seawater. But they are not hurt by this pressure squeeze as humans would be.

Dolphins make clicks and squeals, sounds that others in their group, or pod, learn to interpret. These noises are part of their echolocation system: the sounds go out, strike something in the water, and are reflected back thus locating the object for the dolphin. The dolphin learns to interpret these reflected sounds and swims to avoid obstructions in the water even when it cannot see them. Dolphins also use their echolocation to catch food.

The female dolphin carries its baby for about eleven months until it is developed enough to be born. Then the mother nurses the baby for about one year before the young dolphin strikes out on its own in the great big ocean.

The GROUPER

I magine a 500-pound fish. Some groupers are only a few inches long while others, like the jewfish, can weigh about 750 pounds and reach 9 feet in length.

Groupers, for the most part, are territorial fish. Divers befriend them near their homes in caves and rock crevices, feeding them and watching them as the fish follow the divers like domesticated dogs. From their hiding spots, groupers will dash out, trying to catch and gulp down their prey.

There are about 130 species of groupers. One of the most popular groupers is the Nassau grouper of the Caribbean. They weigh between 9 and 16 pounds and are generally 20 inches long when they become mature at about five years old.

Most groupers have cells in their skin that enable them to change color in order to blend with their surroundings. They also exhibit different colors and patterns during mating season.

An amazing ritual has been observed in the grouper family of fish. They mate only once each year and then only when they come together for a mating aggregation. The fish swim vast distances from their homes in faraway reefs to the same spot year after year and form into the shape of an inverted cone during the height of the mating ritual. Males pursue females fat with eggs, then they come together as both males and females release sperm and eggs into the water where fertilization takes place. The fertilized eggs float around

in the sea until they hatch. Years later the young groupers will return to the mating site where they were conceived. The grouper mating ritual remains a mystery of nature.

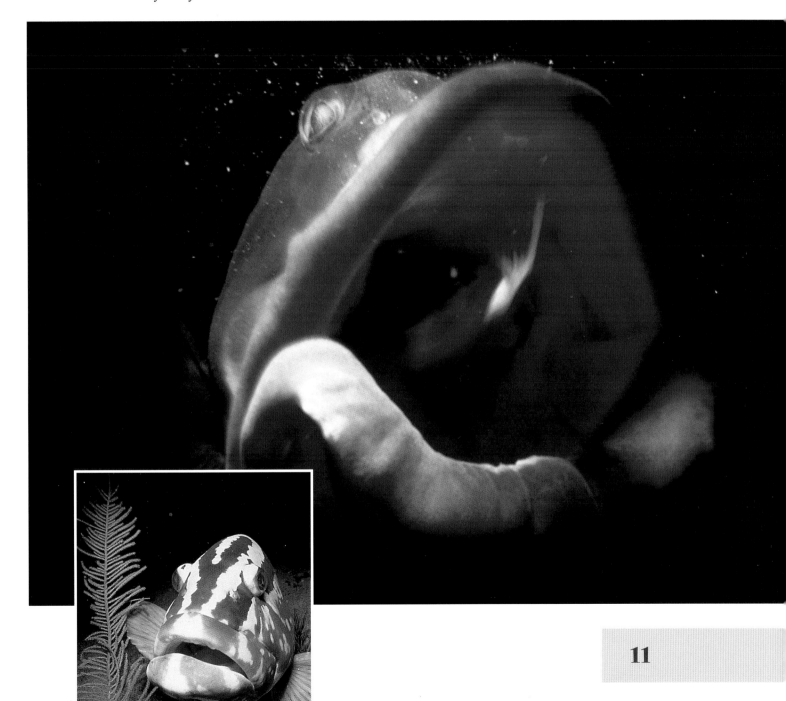

The LOBSTER

How would you like to see a 44-pound lobster? The largest one found weighed more than that and had a 2-foot-long body.

Lobsters have four or five pairs of legs, depending on the species, so they can move easily along the bottom of the ocean. Some species have small fanlike swimmerets on their undersides that help them swim backward quickly to escape enemies. Also, a jointed tail with fanlike sections on the end enables the lobster to flip its tail and swim backward through the water.

Lobsters live in holes or crevices in a reef or inside the remains of shipwrecks during the day. They scavenge for food mainly at night, eating dead or dying small fish as well as live shellfish. Spiny lobsters do not have large claws like their Atlantic Ocean cousins use to crush their food. Instead they have sharp spines over their bodies for defense. If a lobster loses a claw or antenna in a fight, it can grow a new one.

The male lobster fertilizes the female, placing sperm between the last pair of legs on the female's abdomen. The eggs are laid and remain attached to the female's abdomen for almost eleven months. The female protects the eggs and oxygenates them by ensuring that water passes over and around them. When the young hatch, they look like tiny shrimp. Lobsters grow by molting, growing out of their old external skeleton and replacing it with a new one.

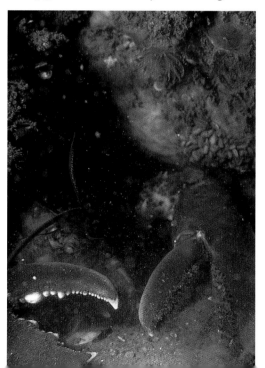

Lobsters belong to the class of animals without backbones called Crustaceans. Shrimp, prawns, crabs, even barnacles belong to this large group of animals that includes some 39,000 species.

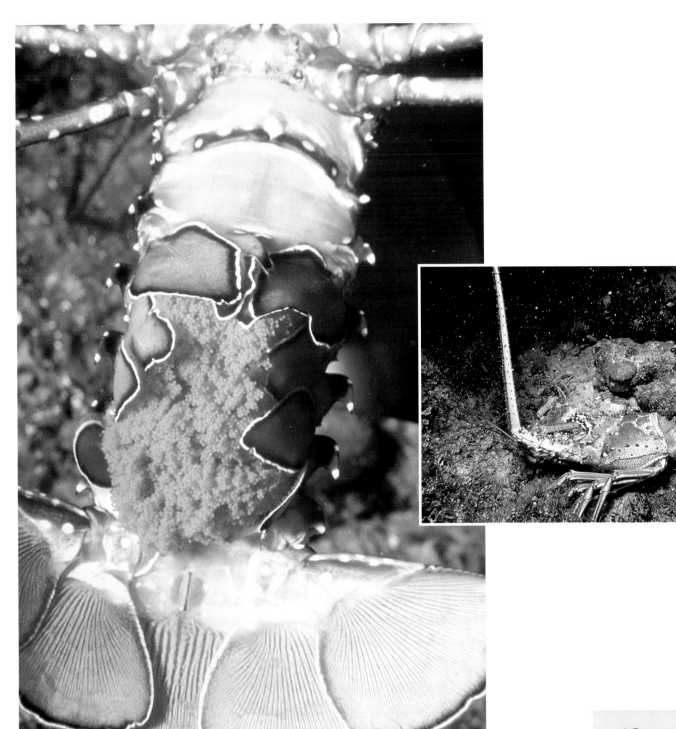

The MANATEE

Can a manatee weigh a ton? Yes. Actually, an adult manatee can weigh as much as 3,000 pounds and reach 14 feet in length. To get that big, a manatee has to eat a lot. It eats only sea grasses, consuming 9 to 15 percent of its body weight in food each day.

These peaceful creatures, also known as sea cows, live mostly off of Florida and in the Caribbean Sea, but their close relatives, the dugongs, are found in some parts of western Africa, the Amazon River, and the Indian Ocean.

Manatees are air-breathing mammals. They take air in through their nostrils, which can be closed tightly when they submerge. Manatees have no external ears but hear via small sensitive areas behind their eyes. They communicate by making sounds, which can be clearly heard by divers underwater.

Manatees can only survive in warm tropical water. However, they must drink fresh water, so even when they migrate down the rivers that flow into the oceans, they must return upstream to drink and rest after a day of foraging for food. In winter when temperatures drop, manatees congregate in areas where natural underground springs feed thermal water to the area. They also stay around power plants where the discharged water is often 10 degrees warmer than the ocean temperature. Manatees are an endangered species; only about 1,800 West Indian manatees survive today. More are killed

each year in canal gates and in accidents with boats than are born. Manatees are not sexually mature until they are nine or ten years old, and when they do become pregnant every three to five years, the female gives birth to usually one calf. Those that do survive can live for sixty years and longer in the wild.

The MORAY EEL

They look fierce and menacing. Their large mouths open and close, exposing fanglike teeth. Green moray eels can grow to be 10 feet or more in length, and their heads and bodies can be larger around than a human thigh. While morays look awesome underwater, a diver is rarely attacked or bitten by one. A bite usually occurs when a diver puts a hand into a moray's cave or disturbs it.

There are about 120 different species of morays. The biological family is called Muraenidae and the moray eel genus is *Muraena*. They get their name from a Roman named Licinius Muraena, who lived in the time of Julius Caesar. Historians report that Muraena kept eels in an aquarium and amused his friends by throwing slaves to the eels to be eaten alive. Because the legend of this early Roman's cruelty is just weird enough, it probably has some degree of truth.

Morays prey on fish and shellfish. A favorite food is the octopus. When a moray captures an elusive octopus, it holds it in its fangs and whips its long body into knots, pulling the prey through the knots to kill it without letting go of its grip, thus giving the octopus no chance to swim away.

Moray eels reproduce by the female laying eggs after she is fertilized. The eggs contain a lot of yolk, which gives the embryo nutrition until it hatches and the baby emerges. Morays develop a mucus on their skin that protects them from disease and bacterial infection.

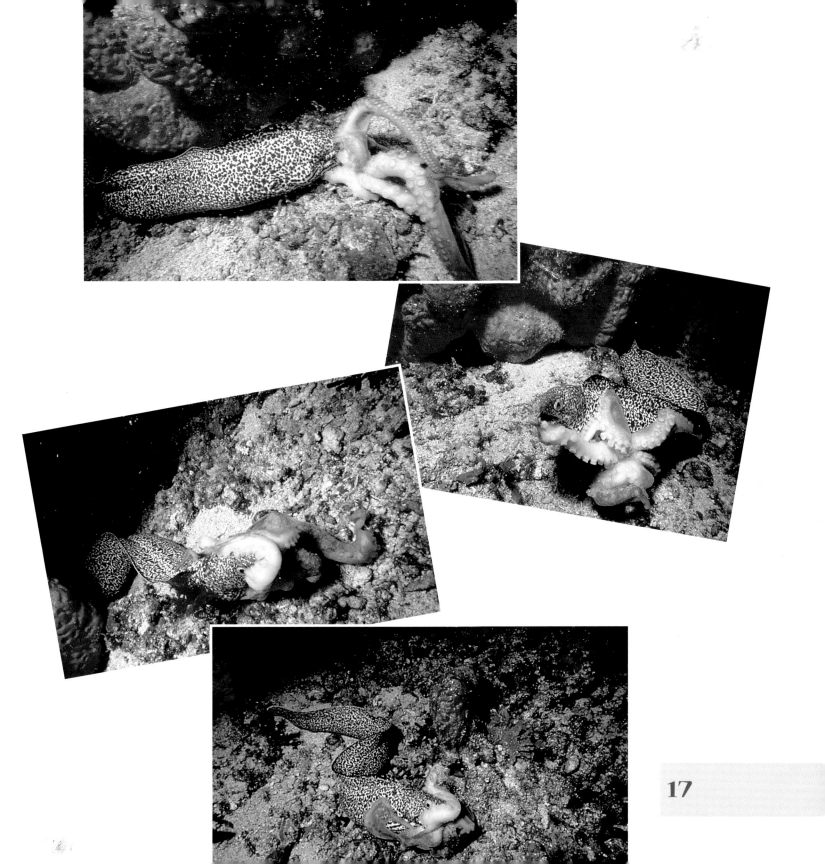

The OCTOPUS

While there are many legends about the fierce giant octopus, it is really a rather shy intelligent creature. It can learn behaviors quickly, such as opening a jar to get to food. Octopuses usually pile rocks, broken shells, or other objects in front of the entrances to their dens to hide. They then come out of their burrows at night to hunt for food.

An octopus's eight arms, with two rows of suckers on each, can grow to be as long as 8 feet each. The giant octopus with a head and body that measures about 1 to 2 feet in diameter, lives in the cold waters of the Pacific Northwest. Other species of octopus are smaller with tentacles that are only about 1 foot long.

The octopus belongs to the same biological grouping as clams and shells. It has no natural shell for protection, only soft tissue and a horny beak located under the center of its body. Octopuses are invertebrates, animals without backbones, and have the sharpest vision of all animals in this group. Watching carefully and patiently, a diver can observe the octopus drawing water in and out of its siphon to breathe and to move.

Color cells in an octopus's skin enable it to change color. It can also change shape to blend in with and into its surroundings to escape enemies. When it feels danger, an octopus can squirt a black ink cloud into the water enabling it to get away. Some octopuses that live near Australia have a deadly poison, and their bite can be fatal.

The female octopus is fertilized by the male's specialized arm, and after she lays the eggs, she oxygenates them by squirting water around and over them and protects them until the babies hatch.

The R A Y

The manta ray, the largest of the rays, has been called the "devilfish" because many people thought the two lobes on either side of its head looked like devil horns. It was also believed that the manta, with a tip-to-tip wing span of often over 20 feet, would descend and lay on top of a diver until the diver drowned. According to another superstition, stingrays could throw the "barbs" on their tails like arrows. None of this is true.

There are about 318 species of rays. Like sharks, rays have no bones, only soft cartilage like the kind found at the end of your nose. Some rays are as small as the palm of a human hand.

Mantas are filter feeders and swim through the water with their huge mouths open, swallowing plankton, small fish, and shrimp. When they are feeding, they spread out the finlike "arms," or lobes, by their mouths to better funnel in food from the water. Manta rays are totally harmless and have no means of defense other than swimming away. They do not even have barbs on their tails, which are shaped like arrowheads. Sometimes remoras, or sucker fish, cling to the manta, looking like fuel pods on an airplane.

Stingrays have sharp spines along the tips of their tails. These "darts" are permanently attached, and on some rays there are venomous pockets that make the barb poisonous, although a wound is rarely fatal to humans. Stingrays have their mouths on the underside of their bodies, enabling them to eat shellfish that they dig out of the sand.

Electric or torpedo rays can stun their prey by sending out a jolt of electricity. These electric rays can give off a 200-volt electric current for about one second, enough to render a diver unconscious underwater.

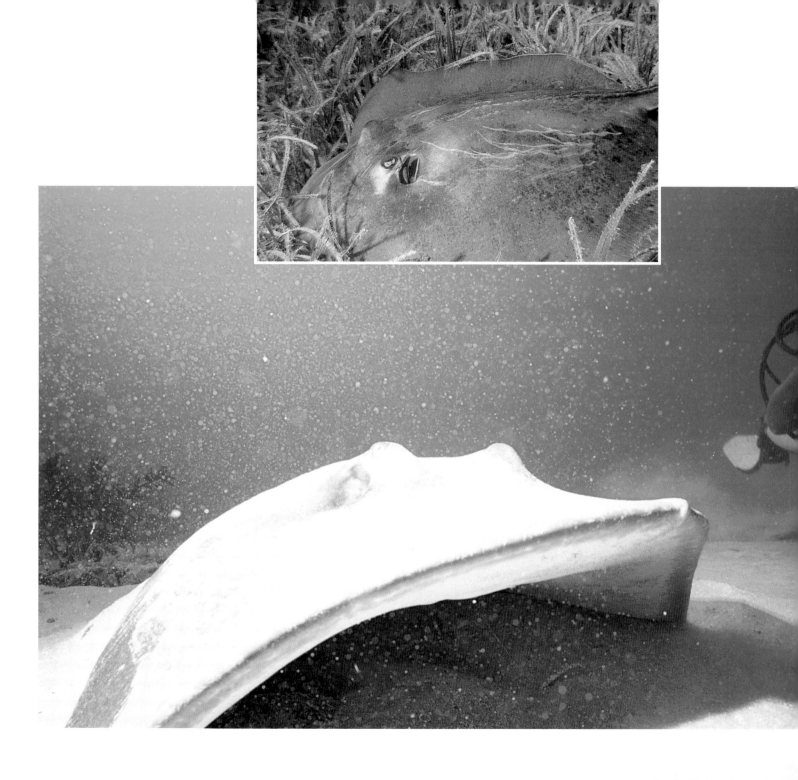

The SEA TURTLE

On land, sea turtles are clumsy and cannot survive for long. In water, sea turtles are among the most graceful of swimmers, using their powerful flippers like paddles. The largest of the sea turtles is the leatherback, which can weigh 1,400 pounds and grow to be 8 feet long. The smallest sea turtle is Kemp's ridley, which weighs only about 100 pounds when fully grown.

There are eight species of marine sea turtles—green, loggerhead, and hawksbill turtles are the most common and are found in the Atlantic Ocean off Florida's coast, the Caribbean Sea, and the Gulf of Mexico. Other species are found in the Pacific Ocean, off Australia, and in tropical oceans. Patterns on a turtle's shell, or carapace, make it easy to identify different species.

Turtles are air-breathing reptiles. They eat mainly sponges, sea grasses, jellyfish, and shellfish such as clams and mollusks. Turtles have no teeth, but crush food with their jaws. The turtle's eardrum is covered with a thin skin, which gives them good hearing.

Turtles mate in the water, then, when she is ready to lay eggs, the female crawls up on the beach to dig a nest at night when the weather is cooler. Often this nest is on the same beach where she hatched her eggs five or more years before. She deposits about 100 eggs in the nest and then crawls back to the ocean leaving the eggs to incubate. It takes about two months for the turtle eggs to hatch.

Construction, dogs, and raccoons all interfere with turtle nesting sites—even human poachers gather up their eggs to sell. Seabirds and the hot tropical sun also kill hatchlings if they hatch during the day. Many are eaten by fish before they can mature. Those that survive drift and float in the ocean, living among large mats of sea grasses, called sargassum, that float on the surface.

Once turtles mature, they have few natural enemies and can live to be quite old. Every so often one is seen with scars on a flipper—the result of a shark bite. The greatest enemy of sea turtles is plastic debris, which they may eat believing the floating plastic bag to be a jellyfish. The plastic gets stuck in the digestive system and death is long and painful. Barnacles bore into turtles' shells, sometimes causing death if they bore into the skull. Turtles are caught in fishing nets and trawls or become tangled in monofilament left by anglers whose lines were snagged underwater. Most species of sea turtle are endangered.

The SHARK

Of course sharks have teeth, lots of teeth. The teeth are arranged in multiple rows and as the front teeth fall out or are damaged in feeding and biting, the teeth behind move into the empty place. Some sharks have as many as 3,000 teeth in their mouths and produce as many as 25,000 teeth in a lifetime. Shark jaws can produce a powerful bite, about 300 times more powerful than the strongest human bite.

There are about 370 different species of sharks. Some are only 15 inches long and some, like the gentle giant of the oceans, the whale shark, may be 40 feet long or more. Some sharks, like the great white and mako, grow to be 16 to 20 feet in length and have no fear of humans. There are fewer than 100 recorded shark attacks on humans each year, and most of those attacks occur in murky water where the shark mistakes the human for food. Sharks are generally timid underwater and it is often difficult to get close enough to a shark to obtain good underwater photographs. Sharks play a very important ecological role in nature, eating dead and diseased animals. They have an undeserved reputation for being ferocious.

Sharks have no bones, only cartilage skeletons, which means they are relatively fragile. If sharks are caught by anglers and then released, they do not always survive as the struggle will have injured their internal organs. Dolphins butt sharks with their strong peduncles, or hard snouts, often causing internal bleeding and death to the shark.

Sharks are graceful swimmers underwater and move swiftly with a stroke of their powerful tails. Sharks have relatively poor vision, and depend mainly on their keen sense of smell, which allows them to detect small amounts of blood in the water even 500 yards away. Specialized cells in their skin pick up vibrations in the water, so they can

sense the vibration of a speared or injured fish at even greater distances.

Sharks do not have swim bladders to give them buoyancy like other fish. If sharks do not swim, they sink to the bottom. Some species of sharks rest in caves or crevices in coral formations. They breathe by using underwater currents or movements of their muscles to push water over their gills, obtaining oxygen from the seawater.

After the female shark is fertilized by the male, how she gives birth depends on her particular species. Some sharks lay egg casings that look like small rectangles with long stringlike tendrils coming out of each corner. These pods may be found empty and washed up on beaches after the tendrils have been pulled out of their anchorages in a reef or the baby shark has been born. Some shark eggs hatch inside the female's womb while other babies develop and grow inside the female's uterus until birth.

The WHALE

What can grow to 100 feet long and weigh 120 tons? The blue whale, which is among the largest creatures on Earth. Tragically, the blue whale has been hunted nearly to extinction, from an estimated population of 33,000 in 1939 to perhaps 1,000 by 1963.

Of the ninety species of whales that survive today, there are two major classifications: whales with teeth, such as the sperm whale and dolphin, and whales with baleen or whalebone, which hangs from their upper jaws. Baleen is a large sweeper or strainer in the whale's mouth. A giant like the blue whale feeds on krill filtered from the water by opening its enormous mouth to gather seawater, closing it, then expelling the water while the baleen traps the krill.

Whale watchers observe different kinds of whale behavior such as lob-tailing (the slapping of the tail fluke down on the water) and spy-hopping (when the whale brings its head up out of the water to look around). Humpback whales often crash their giant tail flukes down on the water, which researchers believe is a signal to other whales. The whalers' cry, "She blows!" describes when a whale comes up out of the water and vapor blows out from the hole on top of its head as it breathes. Breaching occurs when the whale brings its body up out of the water and crashes down on its back with a loud noise and splash. Breaching is also thought to be a means of communicating with other whales and to herd fish for feeding.

Whales, like humans, breathe air, nurse their young on mother's milk, and live in pods or social groups. They are warm-blooded mammals that must

maintain a body temperature of 97 to 99 degrees Fahrenheit, though the water in which these whales live is often frigid. It is the layer of blubber, sometimes 20 inches thick, that provides insulation and keeps them warm.

When a whale dives, its lungs collapse, but the air does not go into the blood and tissues as with human divers. Rather, it is forced into the windpipe and nasal passages as thick linings prevent the air from passing into the tissues. This is how whales avoid the bends, or decompression sickness.

Sperm whales have spermaceti oil, a wax, contained in their heads. This wax melts at about 84 degrees Fahrenheit. The sperm whale's body temperature is 92.3 degrees. When the whale dives deep into very cold water, the wax in its head becomes a solid, helping the sperm whale to dive deeper. As it surfaces, the wax "melts" and becomes buoyant to help the whale rise with less effort.

Whales are remarkable creatures in the ocean world, gentle giants that add to the wonder and fascination of our planet.

Glossary

glôs′ə rē: From the Greek word *glossa,* meaning "tongue" or "language."

Just as the word *glossary* comes from the Greek word *glossa,* knowing the roots or origins of language is very important. Greek and Latin roots form the basis of English and many other languages. Scientific terms and names use these roots. A glossary defines specialized terms mentioned in the main text; some of those terms may not be familiar to a reader. Looking up words in a dictionary and finding their Latin and Greek origins will increase vocabulary and build good language skills, especially for scientific terms.

Here is a glossary of some of the terms used in *Big Stuff in the Ocean.*

Barnacles: Small marine crustaceans that attach themselves to surfaces, including living things. Barnacles have caused great damage to piers where they have bored into and destroyed the concrete. They also attach themselves to turtles and can cause death when they bore into the brain.

Bends, or **Decompression Sickness:** When a diver goes too deep underwater, or stays there too long, nitrogen gas becomes dissolved in the blood and tissues. If the diver then rises to the surface again too rapidly, without stopping at various depths to allow the gas to come out of the tissues slowly, these gas bubbles block blood vessels, killing the tissues beyond the blockage.

Blubber: A layer of fat on whales and other marine mammals. Blubber serves as insulation from the cold.

Breaching: As used in this book, it means jumping up and out of the water.

Buoyancy: Characterized by the ability to float in water.

Cartilage: Fibrous connective tissue. In the human body, it is the soft part of the nose or the ear, in contrast to hard bones, which can be felt in the skull, arms, and legs.

Crustaceans: Lobster, shrimp, or crabs; animals with a segmented body and hard outer shell. These animals are arthropods: invertebrates without a skull or backbone.

Echolocation: A way of finding direction or locating objects based upon reflected sound waves. Humans experience this phenomenon when they shout across a canyon or in a tunnel and hear the sound bounce back off the opposite wall.

Ecological: Characterizes the relationship of plants and animals to their setting in nature or to their environment. Everything has a place in nature, and each species occupies an ecological niche or living space.

Embryo: From the Greek word *embroun,* meaning "something that grows inside the body." The beginning growth of a living thing.

Endangered Species: Species that are on the verge of extinction. Animals and plants that have so few remaining numbers that they are disappearing and are close to extinction (see Extinction).

Extinction: From the Latin word *exstinguere,* meaning "to extinguish." When something no longer exists; when certain animals have died out of existence.

Fertilization: From the Latin word *ferre,* which means "to bear," "produce," or "carry." Biological reproduction occurs most often when the male and female come together to mate.

Filter Feeders: Organisms that strain minute particles of food from their environment.

Genus: The lowest group in the taxonomic classification system (see Species).

Incubate: To warm or hatch eggs; to create a favorable condition for eggs to hatch.

Invertebrates: Animals that have neither a skull covering a brain nor a backbone or a skeleton and cartilage.

Krill: Small shrimplike crustaceans that occur in large numbers in the Polar seas and oceans. Baleen whales feed on them (see Crustaceans).

Lobes: Rounded parts of an organism; a place where the organism is divided into segments.

Mammal: The classification of animals with backbones that have mammary glands to produce milk for nourishing young. The taxonomic class is called Mammalia (see Species).

Mating Aggregation: A place and time when organisms come together to spawn (see Spawning).

Migrate: To move from one place to another to feed or breed, often depending on the season and climate.

Molting: Arthropods (animals without backbones such as insects or crustaceans that are shellfish) have a hard shell or exoskeleton and the animal cannot grow if the hard skeleton remains. When it is time to grow, hormones are secreted that allow the animal to get rid of the old shell and grow a new one.

Monofilament: Made of polymers (plastic), the very strong strand of fishing line that never dissolves and is never destroyed by water. Its long life makes monofilament line a threat to the environment.

Mucus: A lubricating material that provides a protective coating.

Navigate: To travel on a specified course.

Oxygenate: To aerate or let oxygen-containing seawater flow over eggs or through gills to keep an organism alive.

Predatory: A kind of behavior characterized by preying on other animals for food.

Reptiles: From the Latin word *repere,* meaning "to creep." Snakes and lizards are reptiles, as are turtles and alligators. These animals are cold-blooded vertebrates covered with a shell, scales, or horny plates.

Scavenge: To feed on dead or decaying organisms.

Siphon: A simple tube that allows water to enter or leave the body.

Spawning: Bringing forth offspring, usually by releasing eggs and sperm.

Species: Scientists classify animals in a system called "taxonomy" (from the Greek word *taxis,* meaning "order" or "arrangement"), which is the system of putting organisms in categories based on traits they have in common. Species is one of those categories. Organisms of the same species breed together but do not breed with other species.

Suckers: Curved disks that enable an animal such as the octopus to cling to objects. Similar to the little rubber cups used to stick on the wall to hang objects.

Tentacles: Arms or flexible appendages used for grasping prey.

Territorial: Having a specific area or place to live. Territorial animals often defend their "turf" from competitors.

About the Author

John Christopher Fine, a marine biologist with a doctor of jurisprudence degree, is the author of fifteen books, including award-winning books dealing with ocean pollution. He is liaison officer of the United Nations Environment Programme and the Confederation Mondiale for ocean matters and Director of the International Poster Contest for Youth. In 1994 he was elected to the Academy of Underwater Arts and Sciences in honor of his books in the field of education. He has received international recognition for his pioneering work investigating toxic waste contamination of our land and water resources.